Whispers of Love

D1313111

Pat Marsh

To Jacqueline,

with much Love

Carol X

Mizpah.

Onwards and Upwards Publications
Berkeley House
11 Nightingale Crescent
West Horsley
Surrey
KT24 6PD
England

www.onwardsandupwards.org

This edition published 2011

ISBN: 978-1-907509-15-5

First Edition 2003 Foundery Press
ISBN 1 85852 237 4

Second Edition 2005 Inspire
ISBN 1 85852 286 2

Illustrations by Fran Flannery

Cover design: Audri Coleman

Printed in the UK

FOREWORD

Whispers of Love is the story of a journey, 'a love affair . . . growing in silence'. Pat Marsh allows us to accompany her as she explores her experience, returning often to the Cross, and rejoicing in God's love shown in its mystery. Without being too specific about personal circumstances, she writes about being awakened to a deeper understanding of God and herself. Many will find resonances and helpful insights in the freshness and simplicity with which she presents her discoveries.

It has been good to see Pat's writing reaching a wider audience over the last few years, culminating in the publication of this volume. As Pat often says when sharing her thoughts, 'Enjoy . . . '

Ann Lewin

CONTENTS

Restoration

Surrender

Assurance

Celebration

Dedicated to all those who have inspired and helped me along my journey of faith. They are too numerous to mention by name, but it has been my privilege to be touched by their love. I thank them all for the occasions when they have made me aware of God's 'Whispers of Love'.

My poetry is born from prayer,
is in itself a prayer;
and through the tumbling of the words
onto the printed page
seeps
into the stillness of my soul
and leads me deeper
into prayer.

Personal Trials

Not an Easy Option

Stirring the easy slumbers
of my consciousness,
he jolts me
from the cosy rut
I'd channelled for myself.
Breaking the mould of others' expectations,
he questions once more
the status quo in me.
Prompting me to steer my route
across uncharted ground,
he challenges me
to set my feet on pathways new.

It's not an easy option, following God.

For he calls me in directions
where I had not thought to go,
requires of me
a courage which I did not think I had,
turns on their head
my preconceived ideas and plans.

It's not an easy option,
following God.

Darkness

Lord,
be alongside me
in this darkness;
be with me in this fearful blackness
which is so great,
so immensely great,
that it swamps me;
in which I struggle
to know your presence
and nothing
seems real any more.

Lord, hold me.
Help me to know
the comfort
of your loving arms around me,
the strength of your peace
washing over my pain,
the intimate closeness of your presence
by my side
in the darkness.

Lord,
who gave me all I have,
and made me
all that I am,
help me to offer this anguish,
this blackness,
this very great darkness,
into the redemptive power
of your healing love,
and to so lose myself
in your love
that I may find myself again,
in you.

With Care

Try to kill my dreams
and something deep inside me dies.

Trample roughshod o'er my thoughts
and you crush my spirit too.

Fire anger at my longing
and my soul may bleed to death,
lifeblood of my being
leaving me.

But trust me, love me, help me,
respect me and rejoice:
give me freedom to be me
and I will live.

Try to kill my dreams
and something deep inside me dies.

Precious dreams are fragile.

Please handle them with care.

Gethsemane Hour

Deaf
to the shriek
of all but my own agony,
in this Gethsemane Hour
I want no other
than that you should
take this cup away from me.

No lesser response will do.

I can no longer bear the grief
that tears apart
my very soul.

A quest for answers rages within me.

I simply want to know the 'why'
of where I am,
to know you have
a reason
for these wounds, incisions, pain.

But
I am so small
in your great plan
and any answer you could give
would be beyond my power to understand.

I cannot believe
this is your will,
cannot accept this is your plan.
And yet, my Father,
here I am.

Here I am,
in this . . . Gethsemane Hour.
What must our Lord have felt
as he dragged his cross
to Calvary,
where the hammer blow of nails
pierced loving hands
and scarred his naked side,
let flow the blood that was to be
redemptive
for the wounds of others,
wounds of me.

Deaf to the shriek of all but my own agony,
the pain is naught
compared with him who died upon that cross
for me.

And the love beyond all other loves
which raised our Lord from Calvary
looks gently down
on me, his child,
and longs
to lift me from the hurts I feel,
invite me to surrender
to the love redemptive in the Risen Lord,
anoint my wounds
and set me free;

to help me place the screams
of this Gethsemane Hour
within his nail-scarred hands

and whisper quietly
from my heart

my Lord, your will be done.

Caged Bird

Like a caged bird
trapped inside the bars
of others' expectations of me,
singing a false, discordant tune;
I long
to spread my wings,
fly free,
let him lift me
on the thermals of his love,
soar high up in the clouds
in wondrous, free, expressive flight
and sing in harmony
once more.

Hey, This is Me

Hey there, this is me . . .
and I want to say
I'm not the me you seem to think I am.
The person whom you think you see
is none but a reflection
of the image you have built up in your head.
Maybe that's for you the easier way.
There isn't any risk in only looking at
the me you'd like to see.

But I want to say
hey, this is me.

I'd really like to share with you
the bits that you are blind to,
reveal to you the dreams
which you simply fail to see,
help you face
whatever you're afraid that you won't like.
For the me that lies behind
that other me you choose to see
longs to share with you the secrets of my heart,
to skip with you and dance with you
and celebrate the wonder
of the way that we have changed as we have grown.

Hey, look there, this is me.
I can't be any other than the person that I am
and this is who I am
at this moment in my life.

Hey, this is me.

Just look a little deeper, if you can.

Grief

Written a few days before
my mother's death

Grief does not wait
for death
to close the final door,
nor does it wait
for life to turn the closing page;
does not hold back
until the final breath
is drawn.

For grief is here,
and grief is now.

As I observe you starting out
upon your final path,
savour the ecstasy
of the last few
snatched and precious hours,
grief is here,
and grief is now:
in the midst of your living,
the courage of your fragile smile,
in the rare oases of peace,
and in the very heart
of your great pain.

Grief is right here.

Grief is upon me now.

Grief is loving you
with a love that deepens with the grief.

Questioning

You Disturb Me, God

Where are you, Lord?

Where *exactly* are you
in the suffering and the pain
of this cruel, frightening world?

Sometimes, Lord,
sometimes you really disturb my faith.

It's not that I don't believe
that you're a God of infinite, perfect love.
I do. At least, I'm trying to.
It's simply that I just
don't understand.

It's not difficult to see you
in the radiance of a summer flower,
to sense you in the glorious artistry
of a sunset sky.
Far harder to figure out
how to see your hand
in the wretched squalor of the poor
or, worse still, the distended bellies
of the hungry, starving.

Gazing on the wonder of a newborn babe,
I marvel at your gifts.
But looking on the fear and pain
within a cancer riddled body,
I ask myself
where?
where are you then?

Are you at work behind the scared eyes
of the frightened refugee,
the misery of the homeless, alcoholic tramp;
are you active in the tragedy
of the AIDS patient,
or the drug addict barely out of school?

Where are you then, Lord?
It's then,
yes it's then, that I don't quite
understand.
It's then that
you disturb me, God.

Call to Holiness

1 Thessalonians 4:7

Lord, how I struggle
with the challenge of your call.

You call us to be holy.

Inspirational thought that,
appeals to the idealist in me.

You call us to be holy
yet you place us in the world
wanting us, like Christ, to be
right where the people are,
centre stage
in the market-place, as it were,
reflecting your message of love
by the way we live.

Quite simple really,
and yet profoundly difficult.

The message of your Son
was one of love and peace
and of walking in your Word
but all of your creation,
me included,
slips imperceptibly into sin,
cries out
for a brotherly love it does not know.

And I guess that's why
you desire us
to be in this world,
completely in the messy thick of it,
and yet, somehow, set apart.

To say the very least,
that's quite a challenge, Lord.

Your laws are crystal clear
and very much the way I'd like to live,
and I sense, indeed I know,
that were they fully woven through creation
without one hint of sin
your kingdom would be here.

Wonderful thought that.

But humankind
still fails to fully live your Word
and makes a choice to follow self
instead of following you.

The message is so simple.

We are to try to live, completely live,
your laws in every detail.

But there's just one snag in that:
we're clothed with human frailty
and that's the tough bit, Lord.

There seems a paradox there,
as holiness and frailty hold each other
in opposing tension.
But maybe in the contradiction
lies your answer
and your gift.

We need a strength beyond ourselves,
work of the Spirit in us,
to aid the great outworking of your plan.

Without the frailty
we would not need the Spirit.

Without the Spirit
we could not truly know you
as we struggle
towards holiness.

Question Not

My child,
each one must come to me
in his own way
and his own time.

Though I
pour out my love unceasingly
not all have hearts
that are yet open to receive.

And that is not their fault.

You are uniquely you
and they uniquely they.

No other one
has trod a path
that is remotely similar to yours

or theirs.

So question not
why they do not
accept my love.

There are a multitude of reasons.

All are known to me
and I am working out my plan.

Just Enough

Lord, help me
to be content with
'just enough' understanding,
with 'just enough' prompting.

In the infinity of your wisdom
that's what you give me:
no more, no less.
With all the wise discernment of a learnèd teacher
you give me
'just enough'
in answer to my great unanswered 'Why?'
and 'How?'

Still my impatience, Lord.

Don't let the wild entanglement of weeds
which are my questions
smother the gentle
flowering of your love within me.
Don't let their heavy weighing on my mind
stifle creativity
and growth.

Give me humility
to know
that were you to respond in full
I couldn't begin to comprehend
your answers
in their wide, immense complexity.

So let me be content instead
to simply
love the questions
and know that you will give me
'just enough'
to grow, steadily,
one day,
into the answers.

Crown of Thorns

A 'crown of thorns'?

I had not thought it that way.
Thorns, yes,
I'm very familiar with those;
painful, wounding,
nagging in the side of my consciousness;
causing deeper wounds the more I fight the suffering.

Thorns, yes;
but a crown?

Deep wounds of suffering
batter and bruise my heart.
Deep incisions
cutting across all concepts of a loving God;
returning me again and again to
why?
why God, why?

In the infinity of God's wisdom
I am so small
and there seems no answer I can comprehend.

Yet the response to suffering
has been a deep experience
of love, courage, strength, compassion
and, dare I say it, even joy.
An intimate revealing
of God's power to love, transform and heal.
Yes, a 'crowning' of his glory.

A 'crown of thorns'.
I see it now with new perspective.
What privilege to share that crown:
a special peace and joy that none can know
unless they've also walked the path,
the path that means
that only those who've worn the crown
can see the crown on others.

Roller Coaster

Lord, is it always thus,
the call of God?

Have others ridden this roller coaster path
where awesome forces spin their head
and turn their whole world upside down:
one minute sitting on the dizzy heights of joy
and in the next
fast plunging, uncontrollably,
to depths of fear and doubt?

Have others heard your voice,
then heard again,
and known the deep desire to follow you
to be in frightening conflict with
the changes they will need to make?

Have others felt the pain
of recognising all that stands
between the powerful 'yes' deep in their heart
and the flowering
of that 'yes' within their lives?

Have others known this whirlwind of emotions
as they recognise they can't ignore your call;
acknowledge that a mystery
much deeper than can be described
is powerfully pulling them
and loving them towards their destiny?

Have others dreamed of the relief they'll feel
when finally freed
to rest into the joy of that which they were born to be?

Have others wished this path
could easier be?

Lord, is it always thus?

Divine Dynamic

Gracious Lord,
when you called me to follow
I little thought
that it would be this painful,
lonely, hard.

Would I have restrained my 'yes'
had I but known
where it would lead?
Could I have withheld
acceptance of your call?

I know
that I could not.

No ordinary invitation, that,
when you came knocking
in my dreams,
but rather some divine dynamic
calling into being
the beginnings of my destiny.

Could I have withheld my 'yes'?

I know that I could not.

Prayer and Stillness

Spirit of God

Before prayer . . .

Spirit of God,
calm all my fears;
strengthen my thoughts
with knowledge of you.

Spirit of God,
forgive all my sins;
cleanse me, o Lord,
create me anew.

Spirit of God,
empty my heart;
empty my heart,
and fill it with you.

Spirit of God,
peace from above,
descend on me gently
on wings of a dove.

Spirit of God,
come to me now.

Come to me now.
I am waiting
for you.

The Tangled Thicket

Lord, who calmed the raging sea,
still the images
within me;
the complex images which flash across
the hectic forefront of my mind;
a busy thoroughfare
where future plans
collide and jostle
with action replays of the past,
where guilts and fears,
dreams and hopes,
intertwine
with memories and regrets.

Lord, still my mind.

Accept this complex jumble of my thoughts
and make each one
a prayer
as I consciously, tenderly,
entrust each thought
to you.

Create a clearing, Lord,
within the tangled thicket of my thoughts.
Prune out a space:
a sacred space
where there can be
just you
and me.

Create a space within me, Lord,
and fill it with your peace.

Fingerprints

Jeremiah 18:6

Gently working,
potter's hands;
kneading, shaping,
softening clay.
Moulding, flexing,
changing form,
with skilful eyes the guide
to see
beyond the lump of lifeless clay
a vision of what lies within:
potential yet to come to birth,
created from his loving touch
and his fingertip imprints
on the clay.

Lord, let me be
as clay within your hands,
that you may shape
the me you hold within your dreams
and I may know
your fingerprints
upon my life.

Be Still and Know

Psalm 46:10

The silence holds my gaze
in loving adoration
of the stillness which enfolds me,
washes over me,
seeps lovingly into my soul.

The power of the silence
bids me stay;
entranced,
and held.
Embraced.
Embraced in love so strong
that I am drawn
yet deeper still
into the silence;
into unfathomable depths of mystery
and awe,
and inner certainty
that he is here.

He and I are together here,
as one.

A love affair is growing
in the silence.

Less than a Whisper away

Stop, my child.
Stop rushing for a moment.

Put down the complex heavy baggage of your life.
Release your weary grip
upon the endless struggles which you battle with
and try to hide behind.

Dare to let go for a moment
and dare to walk away.

Take time.
    Relax.
        Be still.
Immerse yourself in stillness.

Drink deeply of the silence
and feel
the pulsing heartbeat of your God.

Awaken your soul
to mystery;
reaffirm
the profound simplicity of his love.

Let the intimacy of his love
tenderly embrace you.

Let the warmth of his love
gently nurture you.

Let the joy of his love
enrich you.

Dwell on him in your heart
    and know
        that he
            is less than a whisper away.

Still Point

Lord,
I turn my thoughts
to you.

Within the whirlwind of my day
I stop
and think of you.

It's far too easy to forget you
in the busyness and bustle
of the day,
as other pressures crowd and fill my mind.
And when I pause
I find myself
astonished
that whilst your closeness has been crowded out
yet still
you have been there,
your steady love
surrounding me.

Hello again, Lord.

It's good to reconnect with you,
to take a breath
and feel your powerful presence
in this scene;
enter into stillness
and sense you standing by my side,
shoulder to shoulder in this time, this place,
pouring out your love
unceasingly.

Lord, thank you.

Thank you that you never leave me
even when,
especially when, perhaps,
my temporary amnesia
forgets that you are there.

Becalmed

Journeying
to seek myself,
I fail to recognise the one I find
and, face to face with 'me' once more,
am lost
within myself.

Turned
inside out and upside down,
I bring my broken spirit
to the fragrance of your healing love,
where I can
simply 'be'.

Immersed in love,
embraced in peace,
I come becalmed
beneath the tenderness of your touch
and know
that only a love immeasurable
could heal me so.

Restoration

Fragility

My child,
my precious child . . .
I love you so.

I have my arms around you now.

I feel the fragile, tender,
all-consuming pain within.

I am so close;
and only I
know all that you are feeling.

This moment is a precious, holy moment,
for I am here;
you and I are together here.
And though you may perceive that you're alone,
in fact you're not.

Rest awhile, within my arms,
and I will hold you through,
for I have strength enough for both of us.

Let yourself relax
into the wonder of my peace.

Take courage, child,
for I am here
and all
shall be well.

Yes,
all shall be well.

The Gift of Tears

The dewdrops of my tears
fall sweetly
down my face,
gently wetting my skin
with the tenderness of soft summer rain.

The tears rise up
from a warmth and sadness deep within my soul.

They are not truly mine.
I don't control their birth.
It is a higher power than I
which brings these warm and powerful tears to life.

They are a gift,
and in their falling,
as the soft summer rain
gives life to new shoots from the ground,
so from these healing tears
new life
will spring in me.

Rebirth

1 John 4:18

Conscious of the fears
which distance me from you,
longing to let go
of the hold they have on me,
asking for your blessing
on the prayers I lay before you;

to you,
my loving Father,
I am come.

Nestling in the comfort
of your everlasting arms,
cradled once more safely
in the warmth of your embrace,
giving up my burdens
to your peace.

Acknowledging my fears
in the presence of your love,
surrendering my tiredness
into you.

Head upon your shoulder,
deepening my trust,
tuning in
to whispers of your heart.

Knowing I am precious, oh so precious,
in your sight;
precious child of God
who need not fear.

Waiting in the stillness
for assurance of your Word.

Perfect, loving Father
I am come.

Roots

My child,
though you may not know it
I have brought you to this place in your life
for a purpose.

I have been with you always,
though you have not always known it,
and all that you have been through
has been leading you
to that which you now are.

And all that is still to be
rests safely in my hands.

I love you with a love so great;
infinitely greater than you can imagine.
The love that you have glimpsed
is just a fraction
of the immeasurable love I have
for you.

Like a delicate, tender bud
you hold within you
the secret promise of a beautiful flower yet to bloom.

Allow yourself to blossom, child.

Let the life that is in you
grow as it should.

Put down strong roots
into the richly fertile soil of your experience.
Let me nourish you
with the life-giving water of my love
and sustain you
with the sunshine of my peace.

Trust in me

and let yourself grow
into that which you were born to be.

If Not for Him

If not for him,
the man of sorrows
crucified for me,
I doubt that I could bear this pain,
am sure that
walking in the way of this
my own particular cross
I'd stumble, crumble, fall,
be crushed beneath the weight of it;
be flattened
underneath the thought
that no-one else had ever trod this path
and so could surely not begin to know
the crippling agony inside the pain.

If not for him
I would be trapped beneath the weight of it.

But as I gaze upon the crown of thorns,
so ill-deserved,
the brutal nails so cruelly hammered home,
the blood redemptive flowing from his side,

I know . . .

the man of sorrows
understands.

Surrender

Pain Barrier

You promise that you'll meet us
in the pain, Lord,
and I do believe you do
but sometimes
I just
      can't
           get past

the pain barrier.

Feels like a huge enormous hurdle
I have to scale
before I can get to glimpse you
with clarity
on the other side.

Remind me that you're with me
in the pain, Lord;
your tears, your sorrow,
somehow an integral component.

Save me from the mental gymnastics
of trying to scale the heights of it.

Just hold me
where I am.

Assure me that the pain
is not a barrier
to meeting you
but very much a promise

that you're here.

Utter Vulnerability

When you
were utterly vulnerable, Lord;
arms outstretched
on that lonely cross,
pain
searing through
your bloodstained form . . .

when at your weakest
then you were strongest;
forgiveness
intermingled with the blood,
offering your wounds
in sacrificial love
as you journeyed on
towards the time
of total surrender before the Father;
that point
at which the pain of letting go,
completely letting go,
became the redeeming moment
of being free.

Utter vulnerability.

Total self-giving surrender.

Transforming us
to freely love.

Symbol of Death

Plain, gold cross.
Symbol of death
on a pretty chain around my neck.

Visible reminder
of the friend, precious friend,
who stepped out from the crowd
to suffer and to die,
to pay the price
for me;

for me, for you,
for all humanity.

Anaesthetised by years of history
my heart so easily forgets
that this hand-crafted,
polished,
glistening in the sunlight, symbol of my faith,
symbol of death
on a chain around my neck,
bears no resemblance
to the splintered, bloodied,
raw, rough-hewn reality
of that far cross on Calvary's hill.

Plain, gold cross.
Looks so attractive that my mind blots out
the agonising truth
of that painful, anguished sacrifice
of life, his life,
for me.

Tasteful symbol
of a rougher, rugged, splintered cross
where a dying Jesus hung in agony,
took on his shoulders
all my sin
and died
to set me free.

How . . .
tell me how . . .

how can I do anything
but give my life, my whole life,
back to him?

Lay my Life before You

Help me, Lord
to lay my life before you . . .

Whispered prayerfully
in the quiet
of a contemplative moment
it sounds so simple.

The philosophy
of laying down my life
for you
sounds wonderfully attractive;
if only I could do it.

In the peaceful moments
it feels
like it could be easy.
But when the stresses of my life
crowd in on me from all around,
bombarding me with busyness,
great heaps of problems tumbling at my feet,
then,
then, Lord, it's hard.

Teach me to pause.

Teach me to step outside the mêleé
for a moment,
sidestep the pressures and the troubles
for a while
and in the quietness,
the deep still quietness of my heart,
find you,
and know

that
laying my life before you
is not the desperately difficult act it seems
but rather
can be
profoundly simple.

Freedom

From the deep still centre of my being,
from the very father-heart of love
which underlies and binds the universe,
he calls me.

He woos me with such tenderness;
inviting me,
whispering to me,
challenging me
to turn and follow him.

The choice is mine;
this lover does not force himself upon me.
He knows I have to have the choice,
have to choose for myself
whether to walk the path he shows,
whether to open my eyes to see the signs,
whether to be willing to admit
that I can hear his call.

Freedom of choice is mine.
His signs are there around me,
the stirrings deep within my breast are real.
He can invite me,
woo me, show me (and he does)
but, in his wisdom, he knows
it must be I,
he knows it must be I who makes the choice.

It must be I who dares to take the risk
of trusting in his love;
to take the risk of losing self and be instead
his child,
to be willing to be led
wherever he may lead.

His gift is freedom:
freedom to choose.
He leaves his invitation
open to rejection.

He is asking nothing of me
and yet demanding everything.
For in my heart,
the deep still centre of my heart,
I know that real true freedom
lies in choosing 'yes'.

There is no other choice.

Okay, God

Okay, God,
you've got my attention now.

It took a while, I know.
Lesser folk would've given up on me.
But giving up on people
is not your style,
and all the time
you were quietly there,
knocking,
knocking on the door of my dreams.

You called my name so many times.
So many times I questioned you,
responded with

> Who, me?
> Come on, you've go to be joking, Lord.
> But what about . . .
> What if . . .
> Who . . . ME?
> This just feels crazy, Lord.

So many times I doubted, reasoned, questioned,
had the audacity
to think you'd got it wrong!

But finally,
at last,
I'm listening, God.
Yes okay, God,
you've got my attention now.
My ears have heard your call before,
my eyes have seen your signs,
but now your invitation's reached
my heart.

YES, God.
Please . . . Yes!

Threshold

Lord, how I've longed for, anticipated,
prayed for this moment,
dreamt it in my heart,
even, oftimes, stirred from my slumbers
thinking of it.
And yet, Lord,
it doesn't feel easy,
standing on the threshold
of this new beginning.

Wavering on the threshold of this new start, Lord,
I think I want to thank you.
I stand in awe
of the marvellous way you answer prayer,
although it's rarely how I would have thought,
and never the way
I quietly suggested you might answer it . . .

Forgive my impatience in the past, Lord.
Now that I've arrived here
with clarity of hindsight
I see that you were always close
through all those long, uncertain times
when I was waiting:
waiting for the quiet, unhurried
unfolding of your will.

Standing, poised,
on tiptoe as it were,
on the verge of this beginning;
the as yet untrodden future
lying virgin, beckoning, before;
I sense a moment pregnant with potential,
brimful of opportunity
and hope;

another point where past and future meet
and I may choose
exactly which uncharted path to tread.

And yet I'm nervous, Lord.
The nervousness
is in the starting out.
My eyes keep glancing backward
to the comfort zone of my familiar past.
I am somehow reluctant to begin, for fear I get it wrong,
fail to fulfil the promise within me.

But, thank you, Lord,
that you have brought me here,
albeit by a route I never would have chosen for myself.

Just one more prayer, Lord, if I may:
stay close and lead me on.

C3‍80

My child,
I understand your nervousness,
can see how hard it is
for you to see where I am leading you
when you can't view the detail of the path
from my divine perspective.

Give all your fears to me.
Humble yourself beneath my mighty power.
Keep in mind
that all that lies ahead
is cradled in my love,
held gently in my nail-scarred hands.

I will renew, support and strengthen you.
I will equip you, friend,
to help you live your dreams.

So come now, praise and celebrate
with every fibre of your soul,
and from the threshold of this new beginning
journey on with me.
Step out in faith.
Step out
with me.

Assurance

Son of a Carpenter

Jesus,
simple man.

Son of a carpenter.

No privileged life for him.

Born
into a very ordinary home,
full of the struggles of day-to-day living,
the joys, the strife, the toil
of family life, relationships and work.

Knowing the daily grind
of all that must be done
to make ends meet;
the tiredness
of working 'til his hands are roughened, splintered, scarred;
the difficulties
of balancing needs of others
with his own.

This simple man,
son of a carpenter,
experiencing life
in all its pain,
tempted in every way
to all the emotions you and I might feel.
The pain, the disappointments, anger, hurt;
the stuff of life
that makes things tough.

No easy life for him.

He came
as a simple man,
son of a carpenter,
in every way like us
so we might understand.

He knows . . .

As the Clay

Jeremiah 18:6

As the clay is in the potter's hand,
so are you in mine.

Come, fragile, broken child,
I hold you always in my hand.
Come, let yourself be willing
to be reshaped by my love.

Place all the shattered fragments
of the pieces of your life
within my palm
and let yourself relax
as soft and pliable clay
within my skilful hands.

For I can use all this –
tears, brokenness and pain:
all are the raw materials of my work
to make you new.
Surrender to my warm and tender touch
and I will gently take all you have been
and all you are this day
to sculpt and shape
the you that is to be.

Come, fragile child,
entrust the moulding of your life to me.

So Little Faith

Mark 4:40

Why are you
so afraid?

Have you, my child, so little faith
in him who stilled the raging sea?

Cannot the one who calls you for his work
not calm the inner fears in thee?

Come, you who long to say your 'yes';
leave all the details in his hand,
for when he knocked and called your name,
to help you through was what he'd planned.

I Simply Know

I cannot tell you how I know
that he is here.

I simply . . . know.

Unspoken questions ask me how I know,
and I so wish
that I could give an answer you could comprehend.

But I cannot fully share with you
the peace I know deep in my heart,
because the soul that's feeling it is mine,
not yours.

Nor can I properly tell you how it feels
to be enfolded in his love,
for it is I, not you, that's cradled in the warmth
of that embrace.

And when his spirit gently blows
its tender touch across my life,
I recognise it's me that's standing in its path,
not you.

So I cannot tell you how I know.

I simply know, deep in my guts, that
he is here;

the holy one
is here.

This Holy Ground

Cradled in the mystery
that where I stand
is holy ground,
I rest
in awe.

Embraced
in the truth
that he who loves me
with a love beyond all knowing
is both with me
and within me
in this place,
I rest
in the joy
of being deeply blessed.

He
is in me
and I in him.

What mystery . . .

What precious holy ground . . .

What a gift.

Bubbles and Rainbows

Lord, it's hard
to be open to
the full extent of your love.

We cage our understanding of you
in the limitations
of our own experience,
fumbling
and stumbling with the words
to articulate
the wonder of your love.

It's like
trying to hold a snowflake
in our hand,
or keep a rainbow in the sky,
or catch a bubble
for eternity.

We know it can't be done,
but still we'd like to try.

Forgive us when we wrestle
with the concept of your greatness
and try to measure it
in yardsticks
of our human understanding.

Help us instead, Lord,
to trust

and simply let you love us
into wholeness.

Celebration

Nativity Child

Nativity Child,
awaken anew the child in me.

By the light of the star
which heralded your birth,
light up my life with your joy.

Give me the capacity to see
as a little child sees;
the ability to see the precious jewels
hidden in the everyday moment.
Help me to see with eyes that look upon the world
in simple wide-eyed wonder.

As a young child offers its hand
into the warmth and reassurance
of its father's,
help me to trust in you.

Like a peaceful child,
tenderly cuddled on its father's lap,
help me to nestle snuggly
into the warm embrace of your loving arms.

Help me to celebrate the name
of the Nativity Child
with all the boisterous exuberance of a toddler.
Help me to dance, to sing, to skip,
to simply splash around
in the delight of your love.

As I stride out,
wander off like a little child,
help me to know your eyes are ever on me,
lovingly, tenderly watching me,
protecting me from harm.

And should I fall, Lord,
gently pick me up.

Nativity Child,
awaken anew the child in me,
that in simple trust and wide-eyed wonder
I may let you lead me
into being that which I was born to be.

Gift of a Cross

Forgive me, Lord.
Sometimes I can't quite fathom
why you just can't make
your eternal truths
a little easier to see.

If only your offering to us, Lord,
had come gift-wrapped
on that dark Calvary day,
in sparkling paper
with rainbow coloured bows, perhaps,
instead of the cruel and painful nakedness
of fresh-drawn, still warm, blood
dripping onto rough-hewn wood
beneath a dark, forbidding sky . . .

If only you'd packaged it differently, Lord,
given us the anticipation
of reaching out
to a gift held forth in love;
perhaps then, yes then,
we might more easily have seen
beyond the splinters and the thorns,
perceived
within the wounds and through the blood
that this was not mere horrible injustice,
Jesus' death.
No, more,
far more than that.

Holding the image of the cross
within my mind
I see a sinless human, precious friend,
giving up
his very life for me,

for me and for humanity;
focusing all the agony and pain that we might ever know
on him.
There's comfort, Lord, in that:
to know
the man of sorrows
shares my wounds.

But help me to see the joy within that image, Lord,
to see beyond
the starkness of the crucifixion pain,
hidden inside
this bloodstained snapshot in eternal time,
help me to see
the wonder
of your freely given
gift . . .

that of a cross,

gift-wrapped

in unimaginable love.

Butterfly in a Country Churchyard

Evening shadows lengthen.
Last rays of sunshine
pick out jewelled detail
on the lichened cross
and a masterpiece of nature
rests
upon the granite shape.

Butterfly wings.

Resting in the stillness.
Resting,
fully open;
open to the radiance of God.

And then,
as if on secret breath of evening breeze,
moved by the spirit,
fluttering and dancing in wordless celebration
before returning
gently
to the quiet place
upon the rugged cross.

Miracle of nature
resting
on strong and ageless symbol
of him who loved this iridescent beauty into life.

Father God,
my Lord of the Dance,
revive in me
the joy of the dancing butterfly.

In the death throes
of each ending
I am called to face,
the waiting in the dark
as you bring to birth your plan,

transform my endings to beginnings.

Cocoon me
in the softness of your love.

Enfold me, chrysalis-like,
within your strength.

Enable me to grow
towards new birth,
that in your way and in your time
I too may freely dance
with steps in tune with you.

And in the rhythm of my days
compel me by your fragrance
again

and again

and again

to quiet expectant waiting
in the shelter of your cross.

Dancing in Me

Lamentations 3:22

Love unending
  gift freely given
    bringing its healing,
healing for me.

Love unending
  constantly near
    always abiding,
abiding with me.

Love unending
  misunderstood
    led to a death,
led there by me.

Love unending
  hung on a cross
    quietly dying,
dying for me.

Love unending
  close by my side
    secretly walking,
walking with me.

Love unending
  risen and free
    joyously dancing,
dancing in me.

Who is this Child . . .

After prayer . . .

Who is this child,
so much at peace,
so steeped in love,
so still,
so calm?

Where is the child who broke her heart
with weeping, painful weeping;
who laid her grief before you
with an honesty which hurt;
the child who thought the tears would never stop.
Where is she now?

Who is this child,
so much at peace,
so steeped in love,
so still,
so calm?

I am that child,
renewed by love.